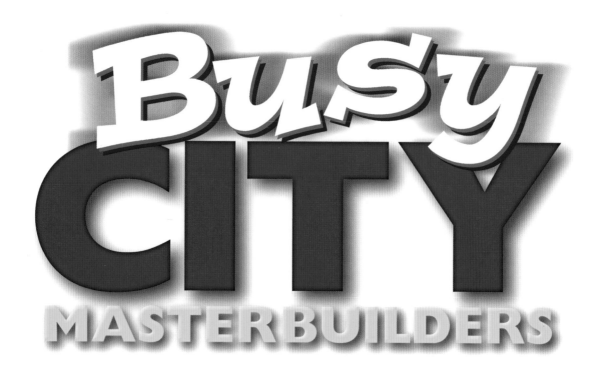

Busy CITY
MASTERBUILDERS

This book belongs to:

....

Age:

....

A LEGO Media Book

 media.

First published in the United States in 2000 by LEGO Systems, Inc.
555 Taylor Road, P.O. Box 1600, Enfield, CT 06083-1600

Reprinted in 2000

10 9 8 7 6 5 4 3 2

ISBN 1903 276136

Colour reproduction by Anglia Graphics
Manufactured in China by Leo Paper Products Ltd.

Check out other cool toys in the LEGO City range!

Busy
CITY
MASTERBUILDERS

Illustrator **Lester Troughton**

Managing Editor **Anne Marie Ryan**

Senior Designer **Stephen Scanlan**

Contents

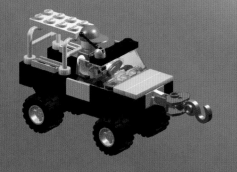

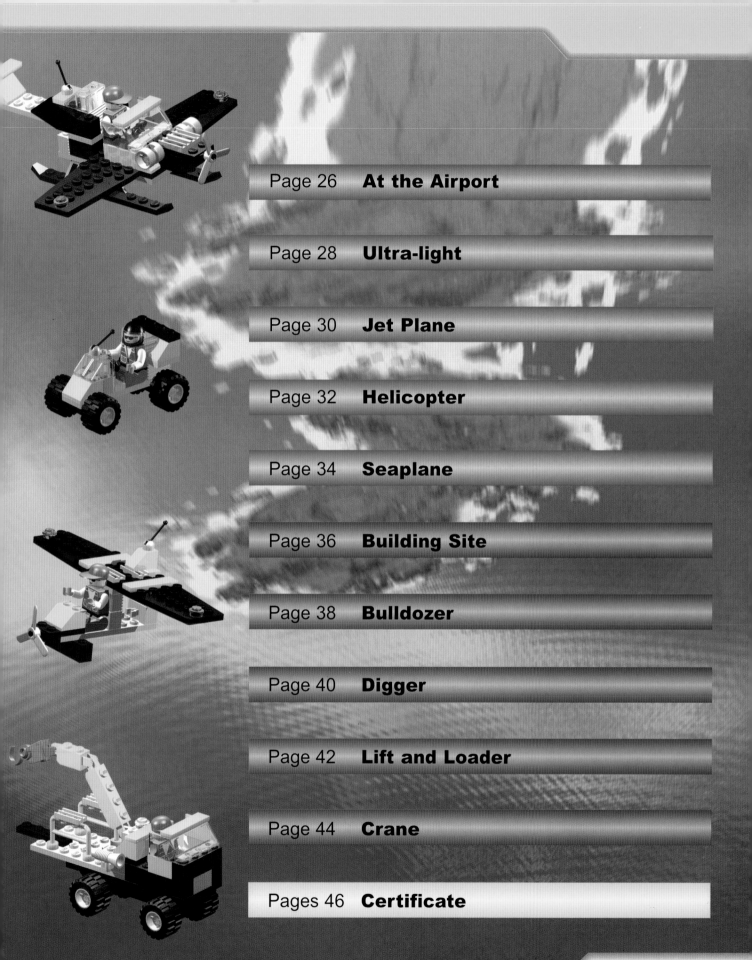

Number of models = 15

Do you want to become a LEGO Masterbuilder? **Busy City** will show you how. Specially developed with the help of professional LEGO model-makers, this book lets young apprentices like you learn from the experts. Work your way through the fun models featured in **Busy City** and you will be a Masterbuilder in no time at all!

The models in this book range in difficulty from easy, to medium and difficult. Try warming up with the simple models before tackling the more challenging vehicles. Special symbols on each page will show you the level of difficulty and how many bricks are used in the model, not counting the Mini figure.

All the LEGO bricks you need to make each model in this book are included in the plastic box. Before you start building a model, it is helpful to find all the LEGO bricks that you will use and place them in front of you. Store the bricks back in the plastic box when you have finished building, so that they don't get lost.

After you have built a model, you can decorate it however you like. The plastic box includes a sheet of stickers, which you can use to customize your vehicles. Give your cars and boats flashy racing stripes, or add chevrons to your construction machines!

There are 15 amazing models to make in this book, but that is just the beginning. There is no limit to the amazing creations you can construct with your LEGO bricks! Just let your imagination run free and you will think of hundreds of LEGO models to build.

Part of the fun of making LEGO models is taking them apart and building something new. Once you have had fun playing with a model, you can turn it into something else! Keep track of which models you have built by filling out the chart at the back of the book. When your certificate is complete, you will be an official LEGO Masterbuilder!

How to use this book:

This box gives you great ideas for playing with your finished model.

These boxes will help you with some of the trickier steps.

10   Sports Car

This lean, mean car sports car rules the road. So rev your engine and start building this stylish buggy! Draw a twisty road on a piece of paper, then drive your car along the course. How well does the car handle the sharp turns and tight corners?

Follow the numbered steps to build the model.

Level

Brick count = 25

11

These symbols show you the level of difficulty.

Find out how many LEGO bricks are used in the model.

Making your Mini figure:

Before you start building models, here is how to put together your LEGO Mini figure. This guy can handle just about any vehicle around — he's an ace pilot, a super skipper and a daring driver!

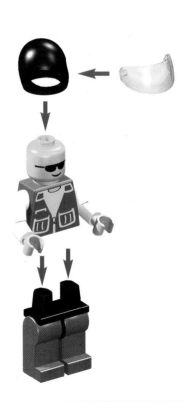

Give your Mini figure a protective helmet for dangerous jobs.

Your Mini figure can also wear a cool cap.

Horns honk, motors roar and sirens wail as vehicles fill the city streets with noisy traffic. Here are three great cars and trucks to build. The only trouble that you'll have is deciding which of these cool vehicles to make first!

Tow Truck

Anybody need a lift? A sturdy tow truck hauls a crashed car to the garage. *Page 14*.

Sports Car
Look mom, no hands! This speed demon rounded a corner too fast. *Page 10.*

Four-wheel Drive
Beep beep! This tough four-wheel drive is in a hurry to head for the hills. *Page 12.*

POLICE

30

Number of models = 3

10 Sports Car

This lean, mean sports car rules the road. So rev your engine and start building this stylish buggy! Draw a twisty road on a piece of paper, then drive your car along the course. How well does the car handle the sharp turns and tight corners?

1

Level

These black bricks make the car's axles, around which the wheels will turn.

You can protect your driver from the breeze with a windscreen made from two clear blue bricks.

2

3

4

Brick count = 25

With double the power of a normal car, this four-wheel drive is the toughest vehicle in town. Its sturdy tires can take on rugged ground as easily as city streets. Test drive your jeep on a steep climb – even mud and gravel won't stop this machine!

2

Position this claw-like piece facing outwards, as you will attach a very handy hook here later.

1

Level

Don't forget to add an antenna so the driver can listen to the radio as he drives along.

3

4

Brick count = 30

13

14 Tow Truck

1

2

Your Mini figure needs to be able to drive, so add a steering wheel to the truck's base.

Level

3

The tow truck has a moveable crane which can bend up and down to lift a crashed car.

4

Tow truck to the rescue! This trusty truck rushes to the car crash to do repairs. This job is too big to fix on the roadside, so the truck will haul the car to the garage using its strong crane. Can you build a car to attach to the truck's hook?

Brick count = 36

16 By the Harbor

Jet Ski
Surf's up! A sporty jet ski is the coolest way to ride the waves. *Page 18.*

Catamaran
Land ho! Slicing through the water, this catamaran sails up to the shore. *Page 22.*

Ahoy, matey! Welcome to the hustle and bustle of the harbor. The Coast Guard watches over all the boats cruising in the bay. You'll have smooth sailing ahead when building these brilliant boats. They are sure to make a splash!

Racing Boat
On your mark, get set, GO! This racing boat is the fastest craft in the harbor. *Page 24.*

Speed Boat
Aye, aye, Captain! A sailor moors his speed boat at the dock. *Page 20.*

Number of models = 4

Bucking the waves like a motorcycle for water, this one-man craft cuts through the surf. Why not build some buoys, then steer your jet ski through a nautical obstacle course? Hang on tight and try not to get wet!

You can start building the base of the jet ski by making a T-shape with two grey bricks.

Level ○

1

2

Bigger boats will see you coming if you add some flashy red and green lights to the back.

3

Remember to attach the antenna, which is partly hidden by the sailor's back.

4

Brick count = 12

The spray of water on your face, the smell of salt in the air, a sea breeze blowing your hair – even landlubbers will love this super speed boat. Why not try adding some cool nautical accessories to make your boat go even faster?

1

To make the boat's base, place this grey brick next to the longer grey brick, but do not connect them yet.

2

Be sure to add the steering wheel, so that your sailor can take the helm.

3

Level

Give the boat a clear windscreen, to keep your sailor from getting wet from the sea spray.

4

5

A boat with skis? It sounds strange but it's true – a catamaran has skis which lift its hull, or body, out of the water. This lets the boat skim quickly over the water's surface for a really smooth ride. Can you invent a catamaran that also flies?

1

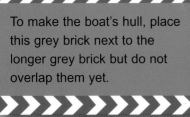

To make the boat's hull, place this grey brick next to the longer grey brick but do not overlap them yet.

2

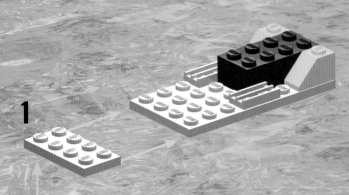

3

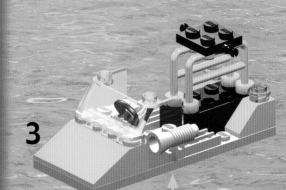

4

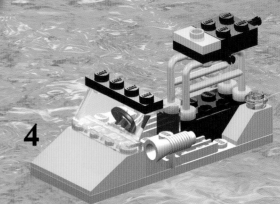

5

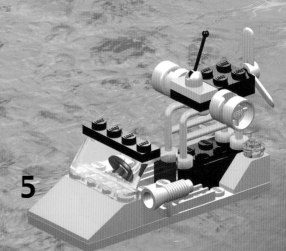

6

Finally, add some finishing touches to your catamaran model and send it on its maiden voyage!

Attach a loudspeaker to the boat's side, so your sailor can call to people on the shore.

Brick count = 29

1

2

3

Though it's hard to see in this picture, there's a steering wheel behind the long yellow bricks.

4

The boat's antenna fits snugly in the middle of the four studs on the grey brick.

5

Your sailor can call out to people on the shore using the loudspeaker at the front of the boat!

6

This turbo-charged boat is sure to win any race. Even a rough, choppy sea won't slow it down. Just how fast can it go? Time yourself as you race to the finish line. The handy hook at the back can help tow slow boats back to the harbor!

The air traffic control tower overlooks the busy runway, tracking aircraft on radar screens. Helicopters whirl, jets taxi down the runway and planes refuel in the big hangar. Let your imagination fly sky high as you build these aircraft models.

Jet Plane

Up, up and away! This jet plane takes off for a long flight at top speed. *Page 30.*

Helicopter

Hold onto your hat! This hard-working helicopter stirs up a wind as it lands. *Page 32.*

Seaplane
The sky's the limit for this seaplane! It glides from the water into the air. *Page 34.*

Ultra-light
This guy isn't afraid of heights! A pilot steers his ultra-light out of the hangar. *Page 28.*

Number of models = 4

28 Ultra-light

Only the bravest pilots dare to fly an ultra-light. There's no room for error in a solo craft! From the pilot's seat, you get a bird's-eye view of the city below. Can you make your pilot a parachute out of a handkerchief and string?

Now attach the ultra-light's wings. The yellow brick on the wings has only one stud.

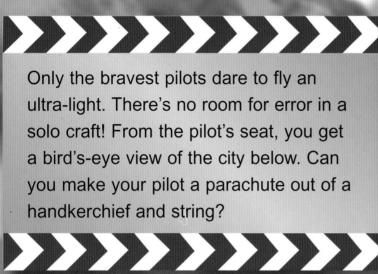

3

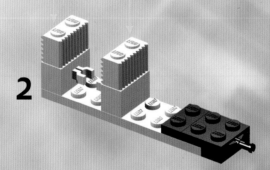

2

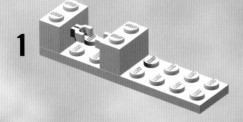

1

Level

4

Add a propeller to the front of the plane. It spins quickly to keep the ultra-light aloft.

Brick count = 23

30 Jet Plane

Fasten your seat belt and prepare for take-off! It takes years of training to become a pilot, but not to build this jet model. Practice take-offs and landings on a smooth surface. You can show off with flashy stunts and loop-the-loops.

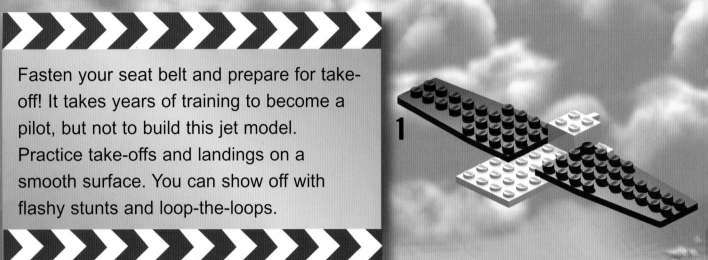

1

Level

2

3

The plane's tail is on a hinge, so the pilot can bend it up and down depending on the wind direction.

Be sure to put a steering wheel in the cockpit, so that your pilot can take the controls.

4

6

5

Brick count = 40

Your helicopter will be seen at night and in cloudy skies if you add red and green lights to it.

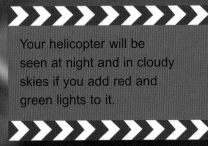

1

2

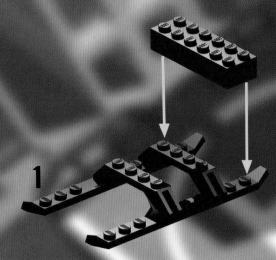

A helicopter can hover in the air and fly in any direction. Best of all, it can land almost anywhere – even on top of a building! This makes helicopters very useful for emergency work. Once you have built your chopper, send it on a rescue mission.

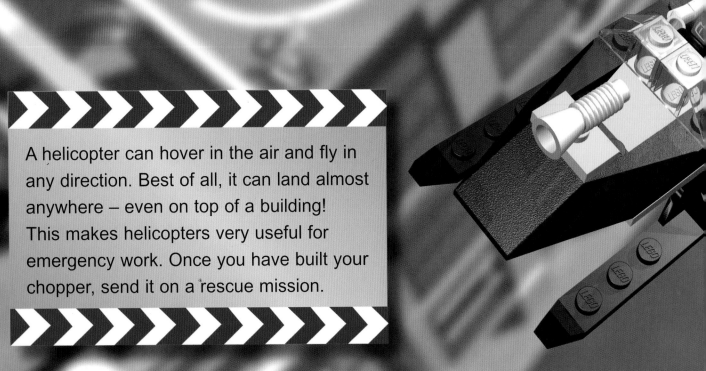

Level

3

4

5

6

A powerful antenna will keep your pilot in touch with the air traffic control tower.

Give your helicopter a lift by adding some rotors to the top and a propeller to the back.

Brick count = 38

34 Seaplane

It's a boat… it's a plane… no, it's a seaplane! Seaplanes have floating skids rather than wheels, so they take off and land on water. Make a big splash by practicing take-offs and landings in a basin of water.

1

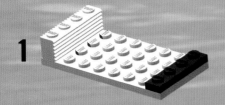

2

Attach a steering wheel inside the cockpit so that your pilot can fly the seaplane.

A clear windscreen will keep the pilot from getting wet during take-off and landing on water!

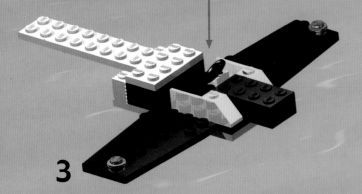

3

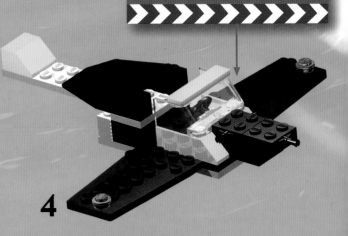

4

Level

Add some finishing touches, such as the skis and a propeller, and your seaplane will be ready for its first flight.

5

6

Brick count = 38

It is never quitting time for the LEGO City building crew. Big, strong machines help the team build new roads and buildings quickly. Now, put on your hard hat and get to work! Once you have made these machines, you can use them to build a whole city.

Bulldozer
Get out of my way! This bulldozer pushes away soil to clear the ground. *Page 38.*

Crane
You'll be hooked on this crane, with its long, bending arm that can lift heavy loads. *Page 44.*

Lift and Loader
Heave-ho! This tow truck carries a long beam to the building site. *Page 42.*

Digger
What's the scoop on this digger? It is carving out a deep hole with its shovel. *Page 40.*

Number of models = 4

38 Bulldozer

Nothing gets in the way of this bulldozer! The biggest rocks are no challenge for this hungry machine. Set up a pile of LEGO bricks and put your bulldozer to work. Now that the ground is cleared, what sort of building will you make?

1

2

Level ⛏

Make a windscreen for the bulldozer by placing the two clear, blue bricks back to back.

5

4

The shovel snaps on to the hook on the grey brick. It can move up and down to pick up a load.

3

Brick count = 26

40 Digger

It digs! It scoops! It hauls! A mighty digger does it all! This digger is filling in a hole so that the crew can build on top. Why not take your digger outdoors and use the shovel to dig a hole? When you finish, the digger can carry the soil away.

1

Level

The yellow arm on the back of the digger is on a hinge, so the builder can move it up and down.

Attach another hinged yellow brick to the digger's arm, to make the scoop even bendier!

2

3

4

5

Brick count = 36

Lift and Loader

The lift and loader truck darts back and forth across the building site, delivering materials to the crew. The long arm at the back of the truck can bend to deliver a load of bricks. Try using a piece of string to attach a load to your truck's hook.

3

2

Building sites are noisy places. Attach a loudspeaker to the truck's side so your builder can be heard.

1

Level

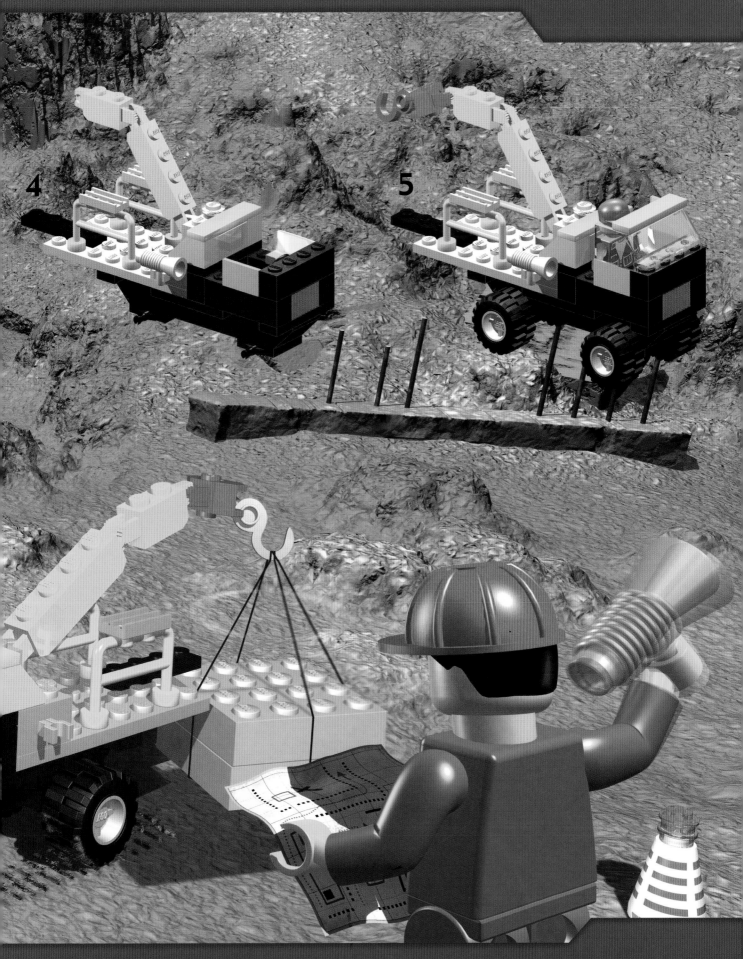

4

5

Level

As the foreman calls orders, the crane driver spins his cab around. He moves the crane's arm and lowers the beam down to the ground. A crane uses its hook and long arm to lift heavy objects. What can your crane lift?

When you complete a model, fill in the date and how much time it took you to build it on this chart. If you make every model in the book, you will become a LEGO Masterbuilder!

Sports Car

Date built: _____   Time spent: _____

Four-wheel Drive

Date built: _____   Time spent: _____

Tow Truck

Date built: _____   Time spent: _____

Jet Ski

Date built: _____   Time spent: _____

Speed Boat

Date built: _____   Time spent: _____

Catamaran

Date built: _____   Time spent: _____

Racing Boat

Date built: _____   Time spent: _____

Ultra-light

Date built: _____   Time spent: _____

Jet Plane

Date built: _____   Time spent: _____

Helicopter

Date built: _____   Time spent: _____

Seaplane

Date built: _____   Time spent: _____

Bulldozer

Date built: _____   Time spent: _____

Digger

Date built: _____   Time spent: _____

Lift and Loader

Date built: _____   Time spent: _____

Crane

Date built: _____   Time spent: _____

Congratulations! You are now officially a LEGO Masterbuilder.